PIXIE LOTT

Delilah Grace

PIXIE LOTT

Delilah Grace

OMNIBUS PRESS

LONDON / NEW YORK / PARIS / SYDNEY / COPENHAGEN / BERLIN / MADRID / TOKYO

Exclusive Distributors
Music Sales Limited, 14/15 Berners Street, London, W1T 3LJ.

Music Sales Corporation, 257 Park Avenue South, New York,
NY 10010, USA.

Macmillan Distribution Services, 56 Parkwest Drive, Derrimut,
Vic 3030, Australia.

PIXIE LOTT

"Such a tiny, cute baby who looked like a fairy."

Budding female pop performers haven't always had the best role models over the past few years. While Amy Winehouse eventually seemed to sell more tabloids than CDs, Britney Spears appeared to plumb new depths of adverse publicity, reinforcing the sense that pop music just might be broken. If it did need fixing, few might have predicted that its saviour would be a teenage Essex blonde – but ever since she exploded onto pop's stage two years ago, Pixie Lott has proved to be nothing less than a sensation.

Although she's only made one album, *Turn It Up*, the singer has already sold well over a million singles in the UK, launched her own clothing range and starred in an American movie. Add to that a sell-out tour, and performances around the globe, and it's difficult to argue that Ms. Lott isn't part of the solution. From her undeniably soulful tones, down-to-earth, friendly persona and looks which, let's be honest, are easy on the eye, Pixie exudes a genuine star appeal and charisma in an age when so many performers hide behind vocoder effects and management Svengalis.

Like many stars who appear to have become overnight sensations, her rise was actually slow but steady, with years of hard work and dedication behind the scenes. Helped by the support of her family and friends, Pixie was allowed to develop her talents at a tender age, away from the public eye, before being unveiled back in the spring of 2009. Perhaps that allowed her to adopt a grounded, level-heaed approach to her blossoming career, which looks set to be a vital ingredient as she enters 2011 with her eye firmly on the main prize of breaking the States.

You could be forgiven for assuming that Pixie was a stage name concocted by some crafty manager; in fact, she was given the nickname by her mum because she was "such a tiny, cute baby who looked like a fairy". She was actually born Victoria Louise Lott on January 12, 1991 in Bromley. The town might technically be in Kent but, to all intents and purposes, it's a suburb on the south-east edge of London. Although it could never be said to be particularly distinctive, Bromley has had quite a reputation for nurturing future talents in the world of popular entertainment, from rock legends like David Bowie, Peter Frampton and Siouxsie Sioux to famous 19th century figures H.G. Wells (the author of *War Of The Worlds*, of course) and Charles Darwin (creator of the groundbreaking tome *Origin Of The Species*).

Actually, Pixie's family were Essex born and bred. Her mother, Beverley A. Martin, married her father, Stephen J. Lott, in March 1987 in Havering, near Romford. The future singer was the couple's third child, joining brother Stephen George (born February 1990) and sister Charlie Ann (born March 1988). Her father was a stockbroker, which probably encouraged Stephen Junior to study economics at college while Charlie eventually became an insurance broker.

By all accounts, the Lotts had no musical tradition in their family – but young Victoria demonstrated an enthusiasm for performing at a tender age. "Mum told me I've been singing since I was in my cot," Pixie explained in 2009, "which is strange because I'm from the least musical family. Ever. I must be a genetic throwback. I was always singing round the house, in the car, literally the whole time."

At her local church primary school in Chislehurst, she enjoyed singing hymns and was enrolled in the Saturday School at the nearby Italia Conti Associate School, part of a network of institutions which

had built up from the original Italia Conti Academy of Theatre Arts in central London, Britain's oldest such training school, which is renowned throughout the world. Every weekend, Pixie started to learn skills in singing, dancing and acting with the Italia Conti team, who were based at Coopers Technology College. At home, she was introduced to her mum's record collection – and was especially fond of hits by Whitney Houston, Mariah Carey, Stevie Wonder and Donny Hathaway, perhaps more than her mum's other favourites, Take That and Diana Ross. Even at such a tender age, Pixie was known to host impromptu performances at family gatherings.

"People would go up to my mum and say, 'You should do something with her', and that's how we realised I had a good singing voice," Pixie later remembered. When the time came to move from primary to senior school when she was 11 years old, Pixie's parents felt confident enough in her abilities to enrol her full-time as a pupil at Italia Conti, where she was awarded a scholarship. At such a vital

period in her personal development, the school provided her with an important grounding.

One of Pixie's first-ever roles on stage was as part of a 17-strong ensemble of sewer children in the hugely successful West End adaptation of *Chitty Chitty Bang Bang*, which opened at the London Palladium in April 2002 and ran for over three years, proving to be the most successful show in the legendary venue's entire history. In 2004, when Pixie was still only 13, the Lott family upped sticks back to Essex – or Brentwood, to be precise, just outside of the M25 and some 20 miles from central London – but she continued studying at Italia Conti.

Pixie's first screen role came in 2005 when she played Louisa von Trapp, one of seven children in BBC1's *Celebrate The Sound Of Music*. Broadcast on New Year's Day 2005, this self-explanatory 40th anniversary tribute to the legendary musical, in which performances were punctuated by interviews with principal members of the cast, was hosted by Graham Norton. Meanwhile, the 14-year-old won a role as part of the chorus line for the recording of *Ça Ira*, an opera created by Roger Waters. Released as a CD in September 2005, *Ça Ira* was a three-act opera about the French Revolution which the ex-Pink Floyd singer, songwriter and bass player had first conceived before Ms. Lott had even been born.

Pixie's heart lay in pop music, though – and her first proper break into the music business came that same year after she happened upon a classified ad which would change her life forever. "I went for an audition in *The Stage* newspaper that was looking for the 'next pop diva'," she later explained, little knowing that this was the very same route taken by The Spice Girls a decade earlier. "I'd always be going through it, looking for open auditions. This one said something like, 'Seeking the next pop diva, age 16-21.' It was for a management deal. I was nagging my mum, 'Please take me', and she was saying,

"Mum told me I've been singing since I was in my cot."

'I don't think you should go, it's probably a con'. She gave in in the end, and there was this huge queue, loads of girls. I sang a couple of Mariah Carey songs, and I got it. From that, I got my first manager. I pretended to be 16 – I was only 14 at the time. A couple of weeks later, I went, 'By the way...'!"

Although she harboured no hard feelings towards her stage school, Pixie was now forging her own path. "[Italia Conti] was definitely more about musical theatre – you know, all smiles and jazz hands and all that," she later admitted. Despite her mum's understandable reticence towards what her official biography describes as "oddly worded, sometimes quite suspicious looking requests for young girls and boys", the advertisement was genuine – and so, patently, was Pixie's talent. Within a few weeks, she was whisked off to New York to set the wheels in motion for her career. Initially, her energies were funnelled into a year's worth of songwriting sessions, expanding on early efforts made at the family piano.

Around 2006, Pixie's demos reached the ears of legendary US impresario Antonio 'L.A.' Reid, a Grammy-award-winning songwriter and producer and a titan in the world of American R&B music. Back in 1989, he had co-founded LaFace Records before eventually running Arista Records and then Island Def Jam. Over the years, the industry mogul had signed and/or steered the careers of such pop giants as Mariah Carey, Pink, Rihanna, Avril Lavigne, OutKast, Kanye West, Dido, Usher and Justin Bieber. Impressed with what he heard, L.A. Reid flew especially to London from his base in New York City to hear Pixie sing in person.

"I just said to my school that I had a dentist's appointment and I came back from the meeting and nobody suspected a thing," Lott later admitted. "So I lied about my age and then I lied about that! Italia Conti is not really the pop side of things, and that's why I had to go out by myself." The audition in a hotel room was enough to convince Reid to sign Pixie to Island Def Jam. "I started recording my album in L.A. at 15 while I was still at school and studying for my GCSEs," Pixie remembered in 2009. "I had to take a lot of time out of school but I managed to get straight As in Dance, Drama, English Lit, English Language, Maths, History, French and Science."

By 2007, a number of Pixie's demos had been uploaded to her MySpace site, attracting wider attention. That included one of the US music industry's most successful managers, David Sonenberg, who'd made his name with Meatloaf's multi-million-selling 1977 album *Bat Out Of Hell* before building a roster for his company DA Communications which boasted such names as The Fugees, Lauren Hill, The Spin Doctors and The Black Eyed Peas. An extremely well-connected individual, Sonenberg helped convince the naïve young singer that maybe the Island Def Jam deal wasn't the most appropriate.

Having canvassed interest from the industry's movers and shakers, Sonenberg's team oversaw something approaching a bidding

war for the would-be starlet. Eventually, Lott signed with Mercury Records in Europe and Interscope Records in North America. Originally a jazz label associated with rock mainstays such as Rod Stewart and Bachman Turner Overdrive in the Seventies, Mercury was by now merely a contemporary imprint within the world's biggest record company, Universal Music.

The last piece of the jigsaw was a deal for her songwriting, which was inked with one of the biggest players in the UK publishing market, Sony-ATV Music, in December 2007. And all this in the midst of honing songs for what would become her debut album. Throughout 2007 and 2008, Pixie collaborated with a plethora of hit songwriters and producers – "bringing out the best in everyone she's worked with," according to her official biography – as well as being schooled in the all-important media training required to be a pop star entering the second decade of the 21st century.

Meanwhile, the pop charts were dominated by a succession of girl groups and female performers. The year's pop phenomenon was undeniably Lady Gaga, the strikingly attired blonde behind such global smashes as 'Just Dance' and 'Poker Face'. The biggest sensation of 2008 in UK terms was Duffy. She too had endured a prolonged gestation for her career behind the scenes before the Welsh lass broke big in 2008 with the retro soul tones of 'Mercy' and the number one album, *Rockferry*.

While relative veterans like Britney Spears and Pink were still riding high in the charts that year, their reign was being threatened by rising stars like Rihanna, and 2008 also saw Katy Perry become a huge star worldwide. Visually, Pixie's blonde bombshell image continued a classic lineage from Duffy and Lady Gaga and that year's other sensation, Taylor Swift, back to Christina Aguilera, Gwen Stefani and Madonna. But was there room for another blonde to capture both charts and hearts?

Pixie certainly thought so. "What's good is that my music is different from everyone else's," she commented during one of her earliest interviews. "It's got the soul element, like Duffy, but it's not very retro. It's a contemporary, pop, fresh sound." In early 2009, Mercury Records were ready to unveil their new charge. Critics were immediately impressed with her soulful singing style, which sounded authentic without relying on the retro stylings of Amy Winehouse or Duffy.

The Brit Awards on February 15 provided the teenager with her first taste of pop hysteria – even if it was a case of mistaken identity. Confusing her blonde locks with those of Lady Gaga, the paparazzi unleashed a hail of igniting flashbulbs when she arrived at London's Claridge's Hotel for the after-show party. "I do quite like it," she admitted a few days later. "You come out of some place and you're almost blinded!"

Although MySpace had afforded Pixie such much-needed early exposure, her choice of social networking outlet in the build-up to her

PIXIE LOTT

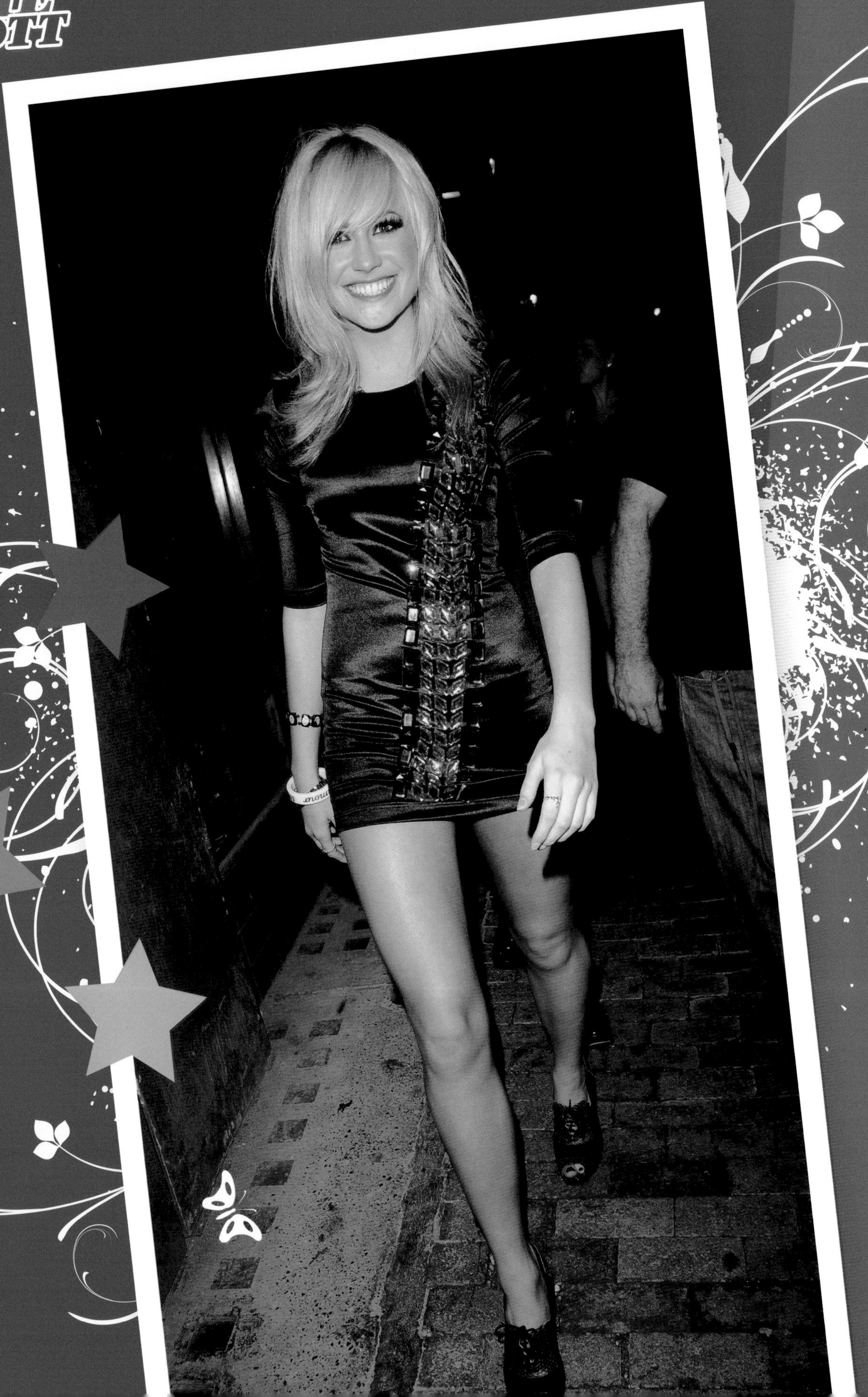

"I pretended to be sixteen – I was only fourteen at the time."

official launch was YouTube via a string of charming video diaries, harking all the way back to her first tentative meetings with industry insiders. Charming and affable, Pixie appeared eminently likeable – and a growing army of online fans seemed smitten by her good looks and happy-go-lucky attitude to *The Sunday Times'* Dan Cairns. The journalist was granted a sneak preview of material from Pixie's now-recorded debut album – and seemed impressed.

For her part, Pixie was keen to emphasise the breadth of her musical tastes and influences, from the perhaps predictable figures of Rihanna and Gwen Stefani (for their style), Britney (for her showmanship), Aguilera (for her commitment), Mariah (for her singing), Lauren Hill (for her spirit) and Alicia Keys (for her songwriting) to older legends of black music such as Whitney Houston, Evelyn 'Champagne' King and Stevie Wonder and indie bands like The Strokes and The Kooks.

Mercury finally unveiled its future star in the lead-up to the arrival of Pixie's debut single on June 6 2009 (its release pushed back from the originally announced date of May 11). The stomping Motown-styled groove of 'Mama Do (Uh Oh, Uh Oh)' proved to be a masterstroke, accurately described by one reviewer as the "archetypal teenage tale of sneaking out on dates under the cover of night", with its naggingly catchy melody and seemingly effortless blend of modern soul and synth-pop. Within days of its upload on April 18, the promotional video had attracted over three million views on YouTube and, helped by strong support from BBC Radio 1, the single duly rocketed to number one with sales northwards of 50,000. (Mercury issued three formats across consecutive days: a one-track download followed by a two-track download and then finally a CD single, a pattern loosely retained for future releases.)

"It's about sneaking out of the house and going to see a specific person without your parents knowing about it," Lott revealed. "It's a really cool song because it suits my age and I can relate to it. I mean, there have been a couple of occasions when I might have sneaked out the house and not told my mum and dad." Pixie had written the song with renowned tunesmiths Phil Thornalley and Mads Hauge, who also produced the recording.

Thornalley's pedigree dated back to the early Eighties. Having worked with legendary Sixties and Seventies producer Mickie Most at his Rak Studios (acting as tape operator for acts like Paul McCartney's Wings and Paul Weller's band The Jam), he briefly joined The Cure as a distraction from his production and mixing work with the likes of The Thompson Twins, The Psychedelic Furs, Duran Duran, Cyndi Lauper, XTC and Sting. Phil also tasted pop fame with late Eighties hitmakers Johnny Hates Jazz, even fronting the band in the early Nineties. After they'd broken up, he'd kept busy as a behind-the-scenes player with Bryan Adams, Ronan Keating, BBMak, Ash, Brian McFadden, Hepburn and The Spice Girls' Melanie C.

Phil's CV might have been extensive but, as a songwriter at least, his name was forever associated with one song, 'Torn', Natalie Imbruglia's huge 1997 breakthrough hit, which he co-wrote. Although considerably younger than Phil, Norwegian guitarist Mads Hauge also boasted considerable experience. Although he played guitar with Girls Aloud for a period, he was best known as co-writer of Natasha Bedingfield's 2007 hit, 'Soulmate' – and he worked at Phil's recording studio, nicknamed 'The Swamp'.

The pair patently got on well with Pixie. "They wrote ['Mama Do'] after we'd had a meeting and I got to know them a bit, after them finding out what I was like and what girls' minds get up to," explained the teenager. "I think it really suits me. I can properly use my voice and it's soulful but yet still uptempo so I can move around and have a lot of fun with it." To promote the single, Pixie was thrown onto a hamster wheel of promotional activity, flitting through numerous TV studios (*Live Lounge*, *Freshly Squeezed*, *Sound*, *Totally Saturday*, *Loose Women*, *GMTV*), radio stations and press lounges.

The gruelling 19-hour video shoot was directed by Trudy Bellinger, who'd had a decade's worth of experience filming acts like Girls Aloud, Louise, Rachel Stevens, Sugababes and Sophie Ellis-Bextor. "It was important to show off all [Pixie's] incredible talents – she is stunning and a brilliant dancer," explained Trudy. "This song has an infectious clap that runs throughout and I wanted to visually reference the clapping and embellish it as the unique hook of the video. The clapping was the obvious starting point... after two days of intense rehearsals, we had an amazingly tight piece, although we had problems with 20 dancers being covered in bruises! In order to get the attitude across and the intensity with the choreography they really had to slap each other. We had to change the styling to hide all the bruises, particularly on the thighs!"

Pixie became the first British female artist ever to debut with a number one – other than those who'd spun off from a reality TV/talent series. "I was in bed at my mum and dad's, where I still live, in Brentwood, Essex," revealed the singer. "I got a phone call from my A&R man. He really dragged it out. I said, 'Please put me out of my misery.' And he said, 'I'm really, really sorry but... you're number one!' I spent the rest of the day running around the house screaming!" Sandwiched between chart-toppers from Black Eyed Peas and David Guetta, 'Mama Do' rocketed Pixie Lott to national fame and was certified silver on August 28 before conquering the Top 40 in many other European countries (it peaked at number five in the European Hot 100). By the end of 2009, it has sold over 200,000 copies and was even adapted in "Simlish" for Electronic Arts' best-selling game *The Sims 3*.

"With competition from Little Boots, La Roux and Duffy, is there room for another big-voiced radio-friendly starlet?" ran the headline.

"*Russell Brand, ... was reported to have approached the starlet during an earlier recording session in Los Angeles with the words, 'You're pretty', only to be shooed away by Lott's mother.*"

24

The answer was clearly "yes". One of the single's accompanying tracks was an appealing acoustic cover of Kings Of Leon's 2008 hit 'Use Somebody', which sold enough as a download to chart in its own right. Pixie's affectionate rendition was refreshingly different from the original, which had featured on the American rock band's best-selling fourth album, *Only By The Night*.

On the back of this spectacular success, Pixie performed a weekend showcase gig at the Wandsworth Palais in London decked out in a provocative black corset and matching knickers. The sexy assemblage prompted comparisons with Lady Gaga – but Pixie's appeal felt closer to the girl-next-door variety, as likely to moan about her struggle with acne as anything else. The tabloids were more concerned with the advances of serial womaniser Russell Brand, who was reported to have approached the starlet during an earlier recording session in Los Angeles with the words, "You're pretty", only to be shooed away by Lott's mother.

On Friday June 12, 2009, Pixie graced her first festival stage in the Big Top at the Isle of Wight Festival. She also embarked on her first string of dates around Britain, supporting The Saturdays during The Work Tour, beginning in Glasgow on June 2. That was followed by trips to Australia, Asia and America for a whistle-stop world mini-world tour. On August 15, she joined Dizzee Rascal and rock bands like The All-American Rejects and Kasabian at Asia's first MTV World Stage Live in Malaysia.

The singer's return to the UK coincided with the build-up to the release of her second single, 'Boys And Girls', which rolled out from September 5. In some respects, Mercury had played safe after striking gold with 'Mama Do'; this was another collaboration with Messrs Thornalley and Hauge and, once again, the team were rewarded with A-list exposure at Radio 1 and a resulting chart-topper, aided by some clubby remixes from electronica duo Moto Blanco. And this despite

some mixed reviews, which suggested that it borrowed from Rihanna and 'I Want It All' from *High School Musical 3*. Other than critics' sideswipes, though, could Pixie's launch have been any more successful?

"It's an uptempo fun song," she explained. "It gives you good visuals because you can just see everyone at the party having fun. As soon as Phil and Mads played me their idea, I instantly liked it because it's one of those instantly commercial songs. Yeah, deffo do that." With its brass and overall vibe, the production hinted at the Sixties soul flavours of Amy Winehouse and Duffy without being so overtly nostalgic – and the vocoder effects on the singer's vocals reflected a widespread contemporary fashion among pop producers.

An early demo version of the song had bubbled up back in 2008. Apparently, Mercury's A&R man Joe Kentish felt that the recording had needed "more drive and urgency and needed to work on the dancefloor as well as the radio". As a result, Mercury had turned to

producer and songwriter Fraser T. Smith, who was fresh from penning hits for James Morrison, Tinchy Stryder and Taio Cruz. "I thought the production was great but felt very retro," Smith admitted. "I wanted to make it a little more current and more urgent – I wanted to make the drums hit a bit harder, and I wanted to make Pixie's voice sound a bit fuller." Ironically, Smith then introduced the kind of old-fashioned brass and trumpet instrumentation associated with Mark Ronson – but it paid off.

Once again, Pixie embarked on a publicity merry-go-round, performing on TV shows like *GMTV*, *Loose Women*, *The National Lottery*, *The 5:19 Show* and *Alan Carr: Chatty Man*. This time, the video (filmed in mid-June) was directed by Diane Martel, a veteran with a background in choreography who'd worked with everyone from Mariah Carey back in the mid-Nineties to Christina Aguilera, LL Cool J, Kelis, N.E.R.D., Beyoncé and Alicia Keys. "It's got a crazy house-party vibe," Pixie said of the video. "There were loads of

interesting extras, weird indie boys and rude-boy gangstas. It's got a dance routine." The result created a more urban/R&B atmosphere than that for 'Mama Do'.

Hot on the heels of the success of 'Boys And Girls' came the singer's debut album, *Turn It Up*, issued in the UK on September 14. Understandably, Mercury pulled out all the stops for the marketing campaign, from a performance at the launch of Blackpool Illuminations on September 4 to a school tour for younger children, Bebo video diaries for teenagers and some Radio 2 live sessions for older listeners. Although the album only peaked at number six, *Turn It Up* continued to sell in quantity for many months, spending five weeks in the Top 10 and over 50 in the Top 40, eventually notching up double-platinum status within a year courtesy of 600,000 units shifted to date. The album also graced the Top 30 in Denmark, Ireland and New Zealand.

However, reviews for the album were mixed. Although BBC Music's Paul Lester offered a qualified compliment in describing it as "a classy, if not classic, debut from potential-rich pop newcomer", he echoed a widespread reservation that maybe some of the material lacked character. Some critics claimed that too many of the 12 songs played it safe and lacked originality, especially the ballads. That said, Mercury wasn't about to take any chances with a new act in whom they'd invested a small fortune. And *The Sunday Times'* Dan Cairns had no such reservations, enthusing that the album was "superior, infectious, expertly tailored pop that, had it been recorded 30 years ago, would very likely now be being praised to the heavens".

Turn It Up boasted an array of contributors, ancillary musicians and aides that ran to over 60 personnel. Many of these revolved around songwriting and production teams such as Thornalley and Hauge, who – in addition to Pixie's two singles to date – also

PIXIE LOTT

"Music is my priority, but I love acting and I'd like to get some more experience in that. It should be really good fun. I can't wait."

contributed 'Cry Me Out'. Two songs, 'Band Aid' and 'Nothing Compares', were co-penned by Toby Gad, a German who was by now a successful player in the music industry based in Los Angeles. Gad made his name co-writing such massive hits as Fergie's 'Big Girls Don't Cry (2007), The Veronicas' 'Untouched' and Beyoncé's 'If I Were A Boy' (2008) – the connection with Pixie being that they shared the same manager, David Sonenberg.

The album's title track was one of three created with producers/ writers Jonas Jeberg and Cutfather and composer Ruth-Anne Cunningham, the others being 'Gravity' and 'My Love'. Hailing from Denmark, Cutfather – real name Mich Hansen – was a prolific behind-the-scenes man who broke through in 1996 with a hit remix of Mark Morrison's British R&B smash, 'Return Of The Mack'. Subsequently, he'd enjoyed huge success with Jamelia's 'Superstar' in 2003 while also working with the Pussycat Dolls, Peter Andre, Christina Aguilera and Kylie Minogue, assembling an impressive CV of productions and remixes spanning nearly two decades, topped by seven UK number ones. Around 2006, Cutfather set up a recording studio in Njalsgade in the Islands Brygge region of Copenhagen after striking up a professional partnership with another local, Jonas 'Jay Jay' Jeberg.

"I think she's a very talented singer," Hansen has said of Pixie Lott. "She's a beautiful girl and she has got a great voice, and she has a strong label and management team behind her as well. It looks like it's really paying off now. I think she's a very cool girl and we used to have a lot of fun. She has been here to Copenhagen three or four times." Ruth-Anne, meanwhile, was a budding singer-songwriter from Dublin, Ireland, who caused a splash when she was only 17 years old by co-writing JoJo's enormous 2006 hit 'Too Little Too Late'.

"'My Love' was the first song I'd written with [them]," explained Pixie. "Great little writing team! They'd been working on [the track] and Ruth-Anne started doing the melodies and lyrics. It's one of my

favourites because it's a really summery vibe, really happy. It's about saying a girl doesn't want to lose her love and it's fun to sing because it's really emotional."

Two other tracks, 'The Way The World Works' and 'Jack', were co-written by Pixie with Peter Zizzo. This New York-based all-rounder made his name in the mid-Nineties via a string of hits written and arranged for Celine Dion before working with Jennifer Lopez and helping to launch the careers of Avril Lavigne and Vanessa Carlton. Pixie had met with Zizzo during one of her earliest trips to the States.

"'Jack' was the first song that I'd recorded when I came to New York when I was 15 years old," explained Lott. "It's so different-sounding and fresh, it stands out. It's got like a Seventies vibe and that little nursery rhyme intro. It was written six years ago by Pete and this Norwegian girl. She used to go out with Zac from Hanson and wanted to write a song about how she could never get over him

but obviously didn't want to call it Zac because he would know – so she called it Jack!"

The writing of 'The Way The World Works' felt like a reunion of sorts. "It was like the first time that we'd got back together in two years," the singer explained. "It was great to see him again because we always have such a good time. Pete's really talented. He'd already had the idea [for the song] and we went into his studio and worked on lyrics."

For 'Here We Go Again', Pixie teamed up with producer RedOne, the stage name for Moroccan-born producer/songwriter Nadir Khayat, who'd relocated to Sweden aged 19. Having tasted chart success as a producer in Scandinavia, RedOne enjoyed wider acclaim in 2006 courtesy of 'Bamboo', the "official melody" for that year's Fifa World Cup, a remix of which was performed with Wyclef Jean and Shakira at the Finals in Berlin to an estimated worldwide TV audience of 1.2 billion. Moving to New York, RedOne created hits for

the likes of Akon and Enrique Iglesias before scoring the big prize in 2008 with Lady Gaga, co-writing and producing her first worldwide hits, 'Just Dance' and 'Poker Face'.

By the time RedOne came to work with Pixie alongside songwriters Steve Kipner and Andrew Frampton, he'd relocated to Los Angeles. Pixie was in good hands. An Australian who'd originally flirted with success as a musician, Kipner boasted a pedigree spanning five decades, way back to his days supporting The Bee Gees in the late Sixties. After spending the Seventies in several bands out in the States, he switched to a backroom role and was rewarded with a global smash, 'Physical', co-written by Kipner for fellow Antipodean Olivia Newton-John in 1981. More recently, he'd co-penned hits for Christina Aguilera (the Ivor Novello Award-winning 'Genie In A Bottle'), Natasha Bedingfield, Kelly Rowland and The Script.

Andrew Frampton came from closer to home. "It was cool because when I first walked into the studio, I'd worked with Steve before but I hadn't worked with Andrew and he's also an Essex boy from Brentwood where I live," revealed Pixie. "It's so weird that we're both in the same room in L.A. even though we're from the same town. ['Here We Go Again'] is really fun. You know when you wake up and you feel really ill in bed and you can't go out but then you think, the only cure for how you feel is to go out again. So you end up being the last one on the dancefloor!"

The album's final track was 'Hold Me In Your Arms', co-written by the singer with up-and-coming figure Ryan Laubscher, a graduate who studied classical composition at the Royal College Of Music before creating his own company, RCW Productions. The song was notable for having been written when Pixie was still only 14 years old and managed, according to critic Dan Cairns, "thanks to an extraordinarily subtle vocal, to be both tender and forlorn".

"Being on stage is definitely the best part. It's such a buzz. I've grown up doing shows, but having my own set and my own band is just amazing. The main thing is just to do amazing tours in front of massive audiences. That and writing songs to inspire people makes me happy."

That acoustic Kings Of Leon cover, 'Use Somebody', was also added to the iTunes download edition while 'Hurt (Sufrirás)', credited to David Bisbal featuring Pixie Lott, swelled the Spanish variation (Bisbal being a major star in his native country). The song also appeared on Bisbal's album *Sin Mirar Atrás* (issued October 20).

Although the teenager must have had a roller-coaster ride making her album, she admitted that her heart lay instead in her live shows. "Being on stage is definitely the best part. It's such a buzz," said Pixie. "I've grown up doing shows, but having my own set and my own band is just amazing. The main thing is just to do amazing tours in front of massive audiences. That and writing songs to inspire people makes me happy."

In some respects, Pixie had put her own personal life on hold, as she revealed to journalist Gavin Martin: "I'm interested in boys, but I haven't really had a proper relationship. I don't know why. I've dated a lot, but I've always been working on trying to do this from such a young age. I've always been in the studio, at auditions and stuff. And at my stage school, most of the boys were gay, so I've got a lot of great gay friends. I was always the girl at nursery school who went in early so I could get the bride's outfit! I would like to get married, but not anytime soon. It would have to be somewhere hot, in a church but with a beach nearby."

In the wake of the success of *Turn It Up*, Pixie was briefly distracted by a string of extra-curricular projects, some of which stemmed from more than a hundred partially self-written songs she had already amassed. One such composition, 'You Broke My Heart', was co-written with producer Steve Booker for Alexandra Burke's debut album, *Overcome*, which was issued on October 19 that year. Two others, 'No Good For Me' and 'Promises, Promises', were recorded by Dutch X-Factor winner Lisa Lois and issued as singles,

as well as appearing on her album *Smoke*. Pixie wrote 'Lonely' for Anna Altieri, a contestant from Italian talent show *Amici*, for the singer's album 9. Pixie also penned the song 'Alone' for budding girl group Girls Can't Catch, which was offered as a Christmas 2009 download on their website (it was slated for the trio's debut album but the band subsequently disbanded).

Meanwhile, Pixie was invited to participate in a hugely worthwhile venture under the banner of Young Soul Rebels, a pop supergroup featuring Tinchy Stryder and N-Dubz. Essentially a reworking of The Killers' 'All These Things That I've Done', 'I Got Soul' was a charity single to raise money for War Child UK. "We're using the track, based around the hook line 'I Got Soul, But I'm Not A Soldier', to draw attention to the 300,000 children who sadly are," explained a spokesman for the organisation. Issued on October 19, 'I Got Soul' peaked at a respectable number 10 and was subsequently performed at that year's MOBO Awards (albeit without Pixie).

For the third single to be plucked from *Turn It Up*, Mercury chose the sultry, smoky ballad 'Cry Me Out', penned by Lott, Phil Thornalley and Mads Hauge with help from Colin Campsie, another experienced figure who'd spent the Eighties in (or working with) bands like The Quick, Giant Steps and Go West. The husband of singer Beverley Craven, Campsie had more recently worked with Natalie Imbruglia, Hepburn and Chantelle Houghton's spoof band Kandy Floss.

"I always prefer to write songs about emotional situations and heartbreak," admitted Pixie, "because I like getting into the character. When we were writing 'Cry Me Out', I said, I feel like singing about something sad but still strong. So the guy has to cry to get over *me*, instead of the other way around. [It] is one of my faves because it's so good to sing live. I want it to actually help people when they're sad and they've had a break-up [so] they can listen to it and be strong. I like that opening line which is, 'I've got your e-mails, you just don't get females, now do you?'." That particular lyric caught the ear of

reviewer Paul Lester, who applauded it as "witty and wise, a masterclass in how to put contemporary language to the service of a sublime melody".

Having been previewed on BBC Breakfast, the single was released on November 22 to reflect a more classy, mature and emotional aspect to Ms. Lott. Although 'Cry Me Out' evaded the Top 10 (peaking at Number 12 in early December), it certainly helped to fuel sales of her album during the fecund sales period in the lead-up to Christmas. Available to view as early as October 30, the single's video had been shot in Cuba under the supervision of Jake Nava, an experienced London-born but American-based video director who'd made his name in the mid-Nineties via promos for Mark Morrison and Shola Ama. During the noughties, Nava served the great and the good of the pop world – in fact, it would be easier to list those chart-topping artists he *hadn't* made videos for. In recent months, he'd worked with Beyoncé, Leona Lewis, Britney Spears, Little Boots and Shakira, for example.

Since much of the video was shot inside a swanky house, it's difficult to understand why Nava chose such an expensive location – but then who wouldn't enjoy a trip to Cuba?! "We had a great time shooting [the video]," said Pixie. "The locals gathered round each scene to have a look, which was funny." Various formats of the single were accompanied by remixes from the prolific dance outfit Bimbo Jones (an alias for producers Lee Dagger and Marc JB and vocalist Katherine Ellis) and Desert Eagle Discs.

On November 4, it was announced that Pixie would be the "face" of Nokia's new range of mobile phones, Illuvial, in an exclusive venture with Carphone Warehouse in time for Christmas. "I spend loads of time on my mobile," admitted the campaign's figurehead, "so it's important to me that it looks good. The phones in the range all look fab – they're stylish and yet still girlie."

PIXIE LOTT

"**What's good is that my music is different from everyone else's.**"

It had been a roller-coaster year for the teenager. Back in January, she was still an unknown quantity, being groomed for her launch into the public eye. Within just 12 months, she'd become one of the hottest names in pop – gracing everywhere from our TV screens and gossip columns to the fashion pages and YouTube. To cap a near-perfect year, a deluxe edition of *Turn It Up* was launched by iTunes on December 21, adding half a dozen tracks to the original 12.

Among them were a version of David Guetta's 'When Love Takes Over', subsequently a huge hit for the producer with singer Kelly Rowland. 'Rolling Stone' was a new song which reunited her with RedOne. "The lyrics are like, 'Another gig to play, a one-hit-wonder song/I want a stand-up guy and not a rolling stone'," explained Pixie. "So it's like saying, this boy keeps coming in and out of my life but I need a proper boy who'll be there. He already had the lyrical idea so it was easy to bounce off of. That day, when we recorded that song,

Randy Jackson came down and I was really surprised. RedOne said [he] was a fan of mine and I couldn't believe it. He was listening to the song, he really liked it. He was giving me advice. It was really inspiring to meet [Randy] and hear what he has to say."

Another new composition was 'Without You'. "I did [that] when I was in LA with Harvey Mason. We went to a studio in West Hollywood, pitch black, no windows, which is kinda good because you just keep working into the night and you don't know that the sun's coming up. The song's about, I don't know if I like it without you, and the melody's really beautiful. Harvey's got a lovely studio but overlooking it is a massive gym because he's crazy about working out. He works out three times a day..."

The son of an acclaimed jazz drummer, Harvey Mason Junior boasted an impressive CV. The Boston-born all-rounder had written and produced for some true legends (Aretha Franklin, Elton John, Whitney Houston, Luther Vandross) as well as more recent superstars like Britney Spears, Jordin Sparks, Leona Lewis and Justin Timberlake. Mason often worked as The Underdogs with partner Damon Thomas; indeed, 'Without You' was co-written with Underdogs associate Steve Russell alongside songwriter and *American Idol* judge Kara DioGuardi.

Another new song, 'Want You', introduced Pixie to Johannes Joergensen and Dicky Klein (who would write for JLS) and Tim McEwan; and 'Silent Night' was a showcase for Pixie to tackle a timeless festive ballad.

Meanwhile, Pixie won a plethora of end-of-year trophies. These included two MTV Europe Music Awards, Best UK & Ireland Act and Best Push Artist; a *Cosmopolitan* Ultimate Women Award for Ultimate Newcomer; The Caron Keating Breakthrough Talent at The Variety Club Showbiz Awards; Best New Act at the MP3 Music Awards; and Best Newcomer at the Virgin Media Music Awards.

Talking to *Cosmo*, which enthused about her trademark look of cute headband, denim hotpants and chunky biker boots, Pixie reflected on her whirlwind rise: "This year has been crazy. Which is such a contrast to before – I've been working on this album for about four years! I was always really frustrated because it was going so slowly, but then as soon as I released my first single, it all went manic! I don't get too fazed by anything and I don't find it hard to stay grounded. I've got great friends and family and it's just the way I've been brought up. I just enjoy everything as much as possible, because as soon as you stop, it's going to take its toll and go wrong. Having a positive outlook definitely helps. When 'Mama Do' was first released, I used to leave the house looking really normal – in a face mask and my glasses. I've learnt my lesson now, though!"

Lott was also questioned about the darker temptations of life in the music biz – and demonstrated a remarkably mature and sensible outlook for someone so young. "I've been offered drugs," she admitted. "I was offered them even before I released my first single. There's loads of it nowadays, but it really doesn't appeal to me. You know how some people start acting like a pop star? They try to be really crazy or squeaky clean. I don't want to be either. I just want to be a normal 18-year-old girl, exactly the same as I was before. A real person. I'll have a drink when I'm out with friends, but not when I'm working because it's bad for my voice."

Perhaps her only vice, if it could be described as such, was a passion for eating at Nando's – and her complimentary discount card at the Peri Peri chicken outlet seemed to mean more to her than the avalanche of free designer clothes that now tumbled through her front door. "I'm in there every day," she confessed. "Seriously, I actually feel a bit embarrassed walking into the branch in Brentwood. I'm like, 'Back again – sorry guys'!"

The singer began 2010 out in Los Angeles, reuniting with Toby Gad to develop fresh material. The visit coincided with meetings to discuss Lott's first foray into the exciting world of Hollywood. For the singer and her mum, that meant a luxurious 10-day stay in a Sunset Boulevard hotel and hanging out in posh coffee bars on Melrose Avenue. "It's really exciting," she explained. "It's great that my first film is a big American one. Music is my priority, but I love acting and I'd like to get some more experience in that. It should be really good fun. I can't wait."

The movie in question was announced simply as *Fred*, based around the character Fred Figglehorn, a six-year-old boy who shares his daily dramas, from a dysfunctional home life to anger management issues. Written by *Family Guy*'s David A. Goodman, directed by Clay Weiner and produced by Brian Robbins and Gary Binkow, *Fred: The Movie* would star 16-year-old Lucas Cruikshank and Pixie would play his girlfriend. The project evolved out of

PIXIE LOTT

"I'm interested in boys, but I haven't really had a proper relationship. I don't know why."

Cruikshank's own caricature, which had taken YouTube by storm – from his high-pitched voice (think The Chipmunks) to his personality disorders.

"It actually just got picked up by Nickelodeon a few days ago," revealed Cruikshank. "Fred's awkward and weird. [Pixie] plays Judy ... the love interest. She's way too good for Fred and [the story follows] Fred's attempts to get to her." Ms. Lott appeared to be taking Hollywood in her elegant stride: "The last scene, we had to shoot with a dog. I was holding a little, tiny chihuahua and in between when we were trying to act, it kept making really weird noises and licking in weird positions. So we couldn't stop laughing."

Back in Blighty, Pixie hit the town in London to celebrate her 19th birthday – but this time, of course, the paparazzi were there to record the occasion for posterity. "The 'Mama Do' singer, who wore a white lace minidress, black leather jacket and a gold headband, was accompanied by a coterie of equally fashionable friends as they

hit the city's most stylish haunts," stated *The Daily Mail*. "After dinner at Cocoon in Regent Street, they hit Boujis in South Kensington. There, Pixie is said to have enjoyed champagne in the club's VIP area before taking to the DJ booth to play one of her own tracks. The group then moved on to Mayfair's Movida before ending the night at 4am at the Soho Sanctum Hotel."

The following week, Pixie graced the stage at the nomination ceremony for the music industry's annual back-slapping celebration, the Brit Awards, where she was in the running for British Single, British Female Artist and British Breakthrough Act. The event was held at London's Earl's Court on February 16 and broadcast on ITV1 – although Pixie didn't actually win any awards.

In the interim, Pixie had headlined at Fight Cervical Cancer In Style on January 27 alongside The Sugababes on a bill that also boasted La Roux and Paloma Faith. This one-off music and fashion event was organised as part of European Cervical Cancer Prevention Week to educate girls and women about the disease. Some 800 lucky fans were granted tickets to the exclusive event, which was filmed and later broadcast on *T4*.

'Gravity' was unveiled as Pixie Lott's fourth single for spring 2010 release, fanfared on February 6 by the broadcast of the video on Channel 4. The glamorous promo was directed by Nick Frew, who'd previously worked with Mark Ronson (directing the video for 'Just'). "So long as Pixie looked stunning I was happy," admitted Frew. "It was liberating, for once, to put beauty first. For the red dot set-up, I wanted Pixie stock still, looking utterly sensational. As soon as Pixie appeared with her black wig, there was a real buzz on set. [She] had the whole crew gathered round the monitor, cooing. It was incredibly satisfying."

"As soon as I heard ['Gravity'], I just wanted to record it straight away," gushed the performer, "because it's instantly a hit song, you

can tell, because the chorus is so massive. It allows you to use your full range because the verse is so low and the chorus is really high. It's a proper belty song so I can put so much emotion in and really enjoy singing it live. It's about a relationship where you want to get away from someone but gravity's pulling you back." Or what one critic described as "love on a bungee rope".

The song was co-written by Cutfather and Jonas Jeberg with Ina Wroldsen (responsible for many of The Saturdays' hits) and Grammy Award-nominated Danish-American songwriter and producer Lucas Secon (who has worked with The Pussycat Dolls, Sugababes and Sean Kingston). While some compared this belter to 'No Air' by American singer Jordin Sparks, others wondered if perhaps the tune was as charismatic as earlier singles. Certainly, its peak position of number 20, following a March 8 release, suggested this was so – despite the potential allure of exclusive remixes from Glasgow-based duo Den Haan and Liverpool quartet Cahill.

On March 26, fashion chain Lipsy announced a forthcoming Pixie Lott clothing line, the latest in a tradition of celebrity-endorsed ranges. Meanwhile, plans were afoot to launch Ms. Lott Stateside, coinciding with the release of *Fred: The Movie* in September. "We are very excited about Pixie's role and we are waiting to see how that develops," an Interscope marketing officer commented, describing a campaign which would be timed for "optimising around the millions of fans that will be exposed to her".

During May 2010, Pixie embarked on a 10-date jaunt as special guest on Rihanna's Last Girl On Earth Tour, winding her way through cavernous venues across the UK's major cities.

Although 'Gravity' had only peaked at number 20, Mercury decided to pull one final single from the album – this time, opting for the title track itself. A month earlier, Pixie was sighted back in Los Angeles filming the video for 'Turn It Up' (premiered on May 6).

While she was out there, she appeared on BBC America's *Graham Norton Show* by way of her introduction to American audiences.

Sounding as if it was influenced by Alicia Keys, 'Turn It Up' was another tune that had been created out in Denmark. "It's about a relationship, how they can't be together but still they know they love each other," she explained, "and I can kind of relate to that." The single was given welcome exposure on the main stage of Radio 1's *Big Weekend* in Bangor, Wales on May 23, *Britain's Got Talent* on June 2, *T4's Hollyoaks Music Show* on June 12 and the *T4 On The Beach Concert* in Weston-super-Mare on July 4. The song reached number 11 after its release on June 7 with sales of nigh on 25,000 units, having been treated to some deft remixes by Digital Dog (the stage name for electro/house producers Steve Cornish and Nick Mace) and Dee-Lux (yet another production duo: Joel Edwards and Robin Axford).

"I spend loads of time on my mobile, so it's important to me that it looks good."

To date, Pixie's career had been the stuff of dreams – and this despite any involvement with TV talent shows. But when Dannii Minogue had to step down as a judge on ITV's hugely popular *The X Factor*, Ms. Lott jumped at the chance to take her place. On July 2, she was spotted attending auditions at the Cardiff International Centre: "I am really excited to be one of the guest judges," she enthused. "It's a new experience for me and I'm looking forward to it. I hope we find some talented singers. I think JLS have definitely paved the way with bands because they're doing really well but I also think that we need a male artist, because they're always my favourites." Asked which song she might opt for, if she were ever to appear on *The X Factor*, she chose 'One Moment In Time' by Whitney Houston.

On July 20, Pixie appeared at the iTunes Festival at historic venue The Roundhouse in Camden, North London. Highlights of her performance included a version of Gladys Knight & The Pips' Seventies soul hit 'Midnight Train To Georgia' (dedicated to her mum) and a medley encompassing some of Pixie's other favourite songs: Alicia Keys' 'Sleeping With A Broken Heart', Jason Derülo's 'Ridin' Solo', Usher's 'OMG', Tinie Tempah's 'Pass Out' and Rihanna's 'Rude Boy'.

While it was announced that Pixie would be performing at that year's V Festival, in Stafford on August 21, the singer was gearing up for her launch across the pond with the impending release there of 'Boys And Girls' to coincide with the Nickelodeon premiere on September 17 of *Fred: The Movie*. Pixie also guested on two recordings by other artists: 'The One' by Stan Walker from his album *From The Inside Out* (issued 31 August) and on 'Live For The Moment' on the film soundtrack album *Street Dance 3D*.

Meanwhile, news reports suggested that, by late summer, Pixie had finally flown the family nest to live in Shoreditch with her boyfriend, the successful male model Oliver Cheshire. She'd also been spotted on holiday in Spain in the summer with friends, including rapper Chipmunk.

In order to maintain the incredible upwards momentum of Pixie's musical career, Mercury opted for a brand new autumn 2010 single to fanfare a new, improved version of her album as *Turn It Up Louder*. The new song, 'Broken Arrow', reunited the singer with Toby Gad and Ruth-Anne Cunningham. The video for what the BBC described as a "stormy, heart-wrenching ballad" was premiered on September 16. It was created by the Canadian-born Gregg Masuak, a long-standing director with a career dating back to the mid-Eighties, who'd made his name making pop promos for The Spice Girls, Kylie Minogue, Take That and Celine Dion.

Masauk had been out of the pop video market for a period. "I've only been back in the ring for a short while," Gregg explained. "This shoot was mental but fun: one single day for a bunch of different performances that included several costume and make-up

changes, a narrative with Pixie and two different guys, a series of
dance routines, and a cluster of different scenarios. Pixie's a director's
dream: she's young, gorgeous, natural, has a terrific sense of style and
self, and loves to try things out." The video was also notable as the
first instance of vehicle product placement (namely, the Citroen DS3)
in a UK music video; and for the appearance of model Alex Watson,
brother of *Harry Potter* star Emma Watson.

On its release on October 10, 'Broken Arrow' peaked at number
12 (again shifting close to 25,000 copies). Alternative versions were
available across the formats, from an intimate acoustic rendition to
remixes from Paul Harris (of Dirty Vegas fame) and hitmakers the
Shapeshifters ('Lola's Theme', etc.).

The single was followed a week later by *Turn It Up Louder*.
Unlike the typical expanded editions of pop albums, which
sometimes offered only an extra track or two, this deluxe version
added nine tunes – although six had earlier graced the iTunes deluxe

download edition. The new arrivals included 'Can't Make This Over', an exclusive composition co-written by Daniel Bedingfield (a successful singer in his own right, of course) with Miami-based songsmith Eve Nelson.

'Coming Home', meanwhile, was a collaboration with fellow rising star Jason Derülo, the Miami-based rapper/singer born to Haitian parents who broke through in 2009 with the five million-selling debut single, 'Whatcha Say'. 'Doing Fine (Without You)' was penned by Pixie with one-time pop star and seasoned songsmith Cathy Dennis alongside her longtime writing partner Chris Braide. The final bonus, 'Catching Snowflakes', was co-penned with Finnish pop star/composer Teemu Brunila. Absent were various covers she'd recorded for radio and TV sessions: Lady Gaga's 'Poker Face'; Evelyn 'Champagne' King's disco/soul classic 'Love Come Down'; OneRepublic's 'Apologize'; and Sinéad O'Connor's 'Nothing Compares 2 U', composed by Prince, which she'd performed on Alan Titchmarsh's show in 2009.

To coincide with the release of *Turn It Up Louder*, Pixie Lott embarked on her first-ever string of headline dates, The Crazy Cats Tour. The 17 dates kicked off in Glasgow on November 24 before winding across England and Wales, including major venues in London, Manchester, Cardiff, Sheffield, Bristol and Newcastle-Upon-Tyne. The shows were rapturously received by the singer's growing army of fans. The most poignant gig must have been a celebratory homecoming show at Brentwood Leisure Centre on November 28, no doubt rekindling still vivid memories of going clubbing with her older sister's ID at the orientally themed Sugar Hut Village on Brentwood High Street.

Looking ahead to 2011, Pixie's second Hollywood film role had already been announced back in May. The singer had been cast in *Sweet Baby Jesus*, a Seventies-themed comedy film based on a modern

PIXIE LOTT

> **"I always prefer to write songs about emotional situations and heartbreak, because I like getting into the character."**

version of the Nativity story in which a man takes his pregnant girlfriend Mary to Bethlehem, Maryland, sparking speculation that the baby will represent the second coming of the son of God. Pixie would play Mary, a role which had reportedly once been earmarked for Britney Spears, for the project created by writer Steve Blair, producer Philippe Rebboah and *Garfield* director Peter Hewitt. Sharing the cast would be Bette Midler (as inn-keeper Eleanor), Adrien Brody, Kim Cattrall (as Mary's mother Darlene) and Sharon Stone.

"Since [*Fred: The Movie*], I got a taste for it and wanted to do more," explained Pixie, who had recently signed with American agency CAA. "I studied [acting] at school and thought I would do it five years down the line, but who am I to turn it down?" That said, Ms. Lott preferred her movies of the edgier variety. "I want to go and see *Nightmare On Elm Street* because I like scary movies," she enthused. "I hate it when you are in the cinema watching a film and want to get out. I like to be roped in and get the adrenaline pumping. My favourite movies are the *Saw* films. The last one I saw I was so drawn in by it, I was crying." Production on *Sweet Baby Jesus* had been due to begin in August 2010.

Looking to the future, Pixie looks likely to build on collaborations with international fashion brands. She performed at the end of a recent Dolce & Gabbana fashion show, while Karl Lagerfeld invited her to be the guest of honour at the Fendi show, and the singer has personalised a special edition T-shirt from Moschino. "I have always loved fashion and it's been so amazing having support from such fantastic designers," Pixie explained. "I like to mix classic and vintage stuff with contemporary and designers. My two fashion icons are Edie Sedgwick and Brigitte Bardot."

Although it's too early to predict Ms. Lott's fortunes Stateside, she could ask for no better label than Interscope to launch *Turn It Up* (with an amended track listing for starters) in the U.S. in 2011. As for

new material, titles for around 50 unissued songs have been published on the internet, some of which Pixie has chatted about in detail – including two that were co-written with the Kansas City-born Grammy Award winner Brian Kennedy. 'Miss You' was a joint venture with Daniel Bedingfield and Pixie herself.

"Brian Kennedy – BK, as people call him – did 'Disturbia' for Rhianna and 'Forever' for Chris Brown, so he's quite hot," enthused the singer. "He's really talented, like amazing on the piano. Brian was just playing and Daniel's so fast and his energy is amazing in the studio, he's crazy, and he came out with all these great ideas. We got flowing straight away [so] it was quite a quick song. It's about how people have an argument and you say things you don't mean but the truth of it is that you miss that other person."

For 'Doing It For Love', Kennedy collaborated instead with Kara DioGuardi. "My mum really likes [that] song," admitted Pixie.

"She always talks about it because the chorus is really feel-good. It's got that old kind of vibe to it. Kara instantly came out with the melody and then we all worked together on the lyrics. I think that whenever a melody or a lyric comes out fast, the songs come out better because it's more natural. The best ones always come out when they're just straight off."

Although Pixie Lott's stratospheric career trajectory has been carefully planned, that doesn't mean it hasn't been the stuff of dreams – but one of the many endearing qualities of the teenager who's only just turned 20 is that, when she isn't dancing around, her feet are kept firmly on the ground. "I just want to stay real and not change from how I was before I was in the public eye," she affirms. "Not try to do anything crazy or pretend to be squeaky clean, just give a good example but not be afraid to make minor mistakes that teenagers learn from. I also believe in young people striving for what they want to do, not be afraid to speak out, to live the life they want and be positive."